Dish, 1720–40. Diameter 352 mm. Note the use of all five available colours.

British Tin-Glazed
Earthenware

John Black

A Shire book

D0227239

Published in 2001 by Shire Publications Ltd,
Cromwell House, Church Street, Princes Risborough,
Buckinghamshire HP27 9AA, UK.
(Website: www.shirebooks.co.uk)

British Library Cataloguing in Publication Data:
Black, John, 1922–
British tin-glazed earthenware. – (Shire album; 390)
1. Delftware – Great Britain
I Title 738.3'0941
ISBN 0 7478 0512 1

Cover: *Three pieces of eighteenth-century British tin-glazed earthenware.*

ACKNOWLEDGEMENTS
Unless otherwise stated, the illustrations all come from private collections, and the author
is very grateful to the collectors, who wish to remain anonymous, for permission to
reproduce them.
Nearly all the photographs from private collections were made by John Sennett.
The author wishes to thank Margaret McFarlane MA MPhil FBA for constant advice and
encouragement, Dr Geoffrey Godden for having suggested that he write this book, and
Louise Pearl for preparing the typescript.

Printed in Malta by Gutenberg Press Limited, Gudja Road,
Tarxien PLA 19, Malta.

Contents

Introduction

Earthenware is a type of pottery that is comparatively low fired and that is porous unless sealed with a glaze, thus rendering it impermeable to liquids. A glaze is in effect an exceedingly thin layer of glass deposited on the surface of the pot, and fused to it when fired in the kiln. Over a thousand years ago potters in the Middle East discovered that by adding some 10–15 per cent of ashes of tin to the standard lead glaze they were able to obtain an opaque, whitish surface which they could proceed to decorate. Hence the term 'tin-glazed earthenware', a group to which maiolica, faience and delftware all belong.

The technique spread to Egypt and Spain with the Moorish potters, and thence to Italy, giving us in maiolica one of the glories of world ceramics. Around 1500 some potters left Italy for Antwerp, where they established a thriving business, but, in the face of the religious persecution and appalling civil unrest that overwhelmed the Low Countries in the sixteenth century, many left for more peaceful places. Two of them settled in Norwich in 1567 and the story of British tin-glazed earthenware had begun. It is not always realised that, until the arrival of these two potters from the Netherlands, no-one had used coloured paints on an opaque ground on English ceramics, though coloured ware from Spain and Italy had been imported for several centuries.

The two potters do not seem to have thrived in Norwich because three years later they petitioned Queen Elizabeth I for a waterside site in London and a twenty-year monopoly of production of paving

tiles, apothecaries' pots and other ware. This request was not granted but they moved to a site in Aldgate in 1570 and the pot house they established there, to which they brought at least a dozen potters and pot-painters from the Netherlands, continued in existence for about fifty years. Then, around 1615, two more potteries were established in London, this time in Southwark, and, again, a number of émigré potters were employed.

The output of these potteries was naturally very greatly influenced by their Netherlands ancestry – how could it have been otherwise, when there was no tradition of tin-glazed earthenware in England, and when the potters either were trained in the Netherlands or had been taught by those who had been? It is therefore often very difficult to distinguish between English and Netherlands maiolica produced at this time, the former being for all intents and purposes a continuation of the same tradition.

In the early decades of the seventeenth century, however, large quantities of Chinese porcelain were imported into northern Europe, starting with the capture of Portuguese ships and the sale of their cargoes in Amsterdam. Oriental porcelain soon became much sought after – both in England and in the Netherlands – and potters in both countries wanted to cash in on it by making it themselves. Not having the secret of making porcelain, they began to copy it in tin-glazed earthenware. A number of technical advances were needed before an acceptable substitute could be achieved, such as using tin glaze on the back as well as on the front, but gradually the traditional maiolica was phased out so that by the end of the

Octagonal plate, 1750–70. Maximum width 226 mm. Painted with oriental floral motifs.

Soy jug, 1760–80. Height 131 mm, diameter 78 mm. The neck shows signs of turning and the base is concave. No spout. For sauce.

seventeenth century it had all but disappeared. The new imitation oriental ware took its place, and this has become known as delftware, after the town of Delft, where production in the Netherlands was concentrated. Although Chinese-influenced delftware continued to be made until the end of the next century, an English decorative tradition grew up alongside it. By 1700 English delftware had become quite distinguishable from that of the Netherlands.

During the seventeenth and eighteenth centuries nine more factories were established in London; some lasted only twenty years, others a hundred and twenty. The last to survive, in Glasshouse Street, Lambeth, continued until 1846, making ointment pots and perfume jars. In 1645 a potter from Southwark moved to the West Country and established a pot house in Brislington, just outside Bristol. This factory, which

Charpot, 1750–70. Diameter 204 mm, height 35 mm. Five fishes round the sides. For potted char, a popular delicacy from Lake Windermere.

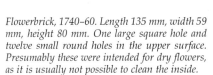

Flowerbrick, 1740–60. Length 135 mm, width 59 mm, height 80 mm. One large square hole and twelve small round holes in the upper surface. Presumably these were intended for dry flowers, as it is usually not possible to clean the inside.

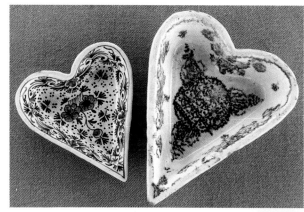

Two heart-shaped sweetmeat dishes, 1750–70. Larger one: length 104 mm, width 84 mm. Smaller one: length 75 mm, width 67 mm. Heart-shaped foot rings, unglazed. These dishes are so shaped that six together fit into a circular surround.

Right: *Leaf-shaped sweetmeat dish, 1750–70. Height 87 mm, width 121 mm. Irregularly shaped, unglazed foot ring. European-inspired landscape.*

Below left: *Puzzle jug, 1750–70. Height 185 mm, diameter of bowl 136 mm. Inscribed 'Here Gentlemen come try your skill / I'll hold a wager if you will / That you don't drink this liquor all / Without you spill or let some fall'. A hollow handle leads to a tube around the top with three nozzles, two of which must be closed before drinking from the third.*

Below right: *Baluster vase, 1740–60. Height 176 mm, diameter 145 mm. It may originally have had a cover.*

Wall pocket, 1750–70. Height 197 mm, width 133 mm. The bird and flowers are press-moulded. Flat back, with two holes for suspension.

continued in production for a hundred years, was followed by others in Bristol itself, which soon became a major centre of production.

The next important centre of delftware manufacture was in Liverpool, where fourteen factories in all were established between 1710 and 1760, producing a great quantity of ware, mostly destined for export to the Americas. A pottery in Wincanton, Somerset, though short-lived, produced interesting work in the 1740s. Two other locations were also important – Dublin and Glasgow; both were in production before 1750 and remained active for twenty-five years or so. The output of Glasgow, in particular, was aimed at the export market. It is not a coincidence that all the important centres of delftware production had access to navigable water, needed for the inward transport of clay and fuel and the outward movement of finished ware.

The production of British delftware peaked in the middle decades of the eighteenth century and sharply declined thereafter, so that by the end of the century it had just about ceased. This decline was due to the introduction of a new ceramic body called creamware and the steady development of English porcelain: unlike delftware, which chipped and cracked easily and could not withstand the thermal shock of boiling water, these new forms of ceramics were more durable and less easily damaged.

It is impossible now to estimate how much tin-glazed earthenware was produced in the seventeenth and eighteenth centuries, but Peter Francis (see Further reading) estimates 44 million pieces between 1723 and 1781 from factories outside London alone. The existence of

Posset pot, 1700–20. Height 230 mm. Posset was a spiced drink of milk soured with ale or vinegar.

Below: Bottle, 1750–70. Height 240 mm, width 147 mm. Water bottles like this are sometimes found with matching basins, for a washstand.

two factory inventories allows us a glance at a frozen moment in the life of a pottery. In 1726 an inventory was taken of the contents of the Gravel Lane pot house in Southwark on the death of its owner, Nicholas Oade. From this we can compute that there were in the factory (in round figures) 33,000 pieces of delftware awaiting firing in the kiln; 10,000 already fired to biscuit consistency; 35,000 finished articles, of which about 45 per cent were perfect and the rest 'seconds'. No breakdown of the ware was given, either by the sort of pieces made, or whether undecorated ('white') ware or decorated. Nevertheless, the figures indicate the amount of work going through a small pot house at any one time.

The second inventory is much more detailed and interesting. This is of the Pickelherring pot house, in Southwark, taken on the death (intestate) of the owner, John Robins, in 1699. More than 105,000 pieces of delftware were on the premises, of which 23,000 were finished and stored, ready for dispatch. The rest were in various stages of production. However, the real interest of this inventory lies in the extraordinary range of pieces listed. Almost everything that could usefully be made in

Miniature mug, 1710–30. Height 50 mm, width 48 mm. Miniature pieces are not common in delftware. (By courtesy of Garry Atkins)

earthenware was represented, often in a wide range of sizes. In addition to the usual apothecaries' requirements, the list includes chamber pots, jam jars (of pound, half pound and quartern sizes), spitting pots, sugar pots, barbers' basins, porringers, saltcellars, all manner of bowls, tea ware, dishes, basins, and so on, to nosegay pots – over fifty different types in all, all with a valuation beside them. A breakdown of 4500 pieces ready for final firing shows that 55 per cent of them had been decorated in colour; 45 per cent were to go out as undecorated, 'white' ware. Whether these percentages can be applied to delftware generally is not known: other calculations have suggested a rather higher proportion of white to decorated ware. Since white, everyday ware was discarded when its life was over, very little has survived, but decorated ware – particularly polychrome – was obviously treasured and retained, and it is not now possible to obtain a better estimate. This inventory gives a fascinating bird's-eye view of a two-kiln delftware pot house in the middle of production, with an indication of the immense range, and numbers, of items made.

Manufacture and techniques

Clays suitable for tin-glazed earthenware had to meet a number of criteria, and above all had to be high in calcium. Such clays (a) produced rigid bodies which were pliable enough to be worked but still held up in the kiln; (b) fired to a pale buff colour easily concealed by the tin-opacified glaze; (c) had an expansion coefficient similar to that of the glaze to minimise crazing, which is caused by different rates of shrinkage of body and glaze during firing; and (d) tolerated a range of firing temperatures as these were not well controlled in early kilns.

Obtaining bodies with these characteristics involved mixing clays, typically a local low-calcium clay with a special high-calcium one which, occurring in only a few isolated places, had to be brought in. Initially high-calcium clays from East Anglia and then Kent were used; later clay from Carrickfergus in the north of Ireland supplied the needs of west coast and Irish potteries such as those in Bristol, Liverpool, Glasgow and Dublin.

After proper mixing and preparation, the clay was formed into the shape required either on a wheel or by pressing against a mould. The next stage was to fire in a kiln to 'biscuit' consistency. If the object was to be sold 'in the white', that is, undecorated, it was dipped into the glaze, fired at around 1000°C, and put on one side for sale. The rest of the ware was decorated after the glaze was dry and then fired at about 1000°C. The decoration was mostly with blue only, although a small number, probably 5–10 per cent of the decorated pieces, were painted with two or more of the five colours that were able to withstand the high firing temperatures. Firing fused the colours into the glaze and the glaze to the body, so that the decoration is neither 'under glaze' nor 'on glaze', but 'in glaze'.

In the early days of tin-glazed earthenware in England, only the top surface was given a glaze with tin: the underneath had a lead glaze, probably for cheapness. From about 1625, with the change from maiolica to delftware, the whole body was coated with tin glaze. At first, ware was separated in the kilns on trivets, which left three ugly marks on the top surface when they were removed after firing as some glaze always came away with them. Later on, objects were fired in saggars, resting on pins. When these pins were removed they left three characteristic but much less unsightly marks on the underside.

Five colours were available to the pot-painter. **Blue** came from cobalt and was by far the most frequently used – only about 3 per cent of all decorated ware did not incorporate blue – and it was easy to

Small bowl, 1720–40. Diameter 162 mm. Showing use of blue pigment derived from cobalt.

11

Above left: *Plate, 1720–40. Diameter 227 mm. Showing use of purple pigment derived from manganese.*
Above right: *Dish with fluted rim, 1700–20. Diameter 288 mm. Showing use of red pigment derived from iron, in carefully painted decoration.*

use. The shade of blue varied according to the fineness of preparation, from pale to a dark inky colour. **Purple**, from manganese, was also user-friendly and reliable; blue and purple were often used together, and went very well. **Red**, from iron, always gave problems: it was liable not to fuse into the glaze and can often be felt as a raised lump on the surface. As it was not then covered by glaze, it was liable to absorb dirt and other colours. In the eighteenth century the preparation of red pigment was greatly

Below left: *Plate, 1750–70. Diameter 220 mm. Showing improved, smoothly flowing red and blue pigments.*
Below right: *Plate, 1750–70. Diameter 226 mm. Showing use of yellow pigment derived from antimony.*

Above left: *Charger, 1690–1710. Diameter 343 mm. Showing use of green pigment derived from copper. Tulip design, with blue dash border. Clear lead glaze on reverse.*

Above right: *Dish, 1750–70. Diameter 345 mm. Showing use of mixed green (blue and yellow).*

improved, and smoothly flowing reds could be achieved. **Yellow** was derived from antimony and went very pale if overfired; in colour it could vary from lemon to canary. The most difficult colour to use was **green**, which came from copper. It could turn into a pale wash rather than a strong colour and was liable to creep. From around 1700 green from copper was increasingly replaced by a mixture of blue and yellow, which was not only very much more reliable but also offered a range of shades, depending on the

Below left: *Plate, 1770–90. Diameter 232 mm. Showing use of purple mixed (probably) with blue to obtain a near black.*

Below right: *Plate, 1750–70. Diameter 217 mm. Showing use of all five colours available to the painter.*

Plate with deep well, 1760–80. Diameter 223 mm. Painted in the 'Fazackerly' palette, typically lemon yellow, sage green, dark blue and foxy red, with stems and leaf venation in purple-black.

proportions used. The only other use of mixing colours was the addition of blue to purple to obtain a near black. In this respect, practice in Great Britain was markedly different from that of the Italian maiolica painters, who, although similarly restricted to the same five colours, used them in a much more sensitive way.

Painting on the highly absorbent tin glaze was like painting on blotting paper. The pigments sank in immediately and there was no possibility of correcting mistakes. It required quick, positive brush strokes, often to outline an area that could be filled in later. As pigments and techniques improved, very delicate work could be

Three plates showing unusual and striking use of colours. (Left) 1750–70; diameter 219 mm. (Centre) 1740–60; diameter 216 mm. (Right) 1750–70; diameter 227 mm.

Above left: *Plate, 1710–30. Diameter 210 mm.*

Above right: *The reverse has a rapidly drawn outline of the figure at 7 o'clock on the front, showing the method of working; the outline would then be filled in.*

achieved, but much run-of-the-mill production was rather hastily painted.

A lot of the decoration seems to have been done on a turntable, and this accounts for the popularity of circles and spirals. Reiterative border patterns, too, seem to have been done similarly, as they are irregular and obviously not marked out carefully first. Most decoration was freehand, though there is evidence of pouncing, that

Two contrasting plates, both 1750–70. (Left) Crudely decorated plate, diameter 226 mm. Note that when painting the circles, the painter allowed his brush to run dry before replenishing it. (Right) Delicately decorated plate, with 'bianco sopra bianco' border.

Left: *Plate, 1730–50. Diameter 226 mm. Showing use of a turntable to paint circles, and also delicate 'quill' work.*

Right: *Plate, 1760–80. Diameter 224 mm. Showing use of a turntable to paint a spiral.*

Below: *Plate, 1760–80. Diameter 217 mm. Note the shepherd <u>not</u> sitting on the bank owing to incorrect placing of the stencil.*

is, marking out the design by using perforated paper patterns and charcoal (which would burn off in the kiln).

Most decoration was made with brushes of various sizes and shapes, but other methods were used, such as sponging, for foliage and other special effects. Tapping wet pigment from a brush on to a glazed surface produced a speckled effect: this was used mostly in the seventeenth century, but a refinement of the method – dry rather than wet powdered pigment being blown on to the glaze – was popular in the 1740s and 1750s. Usually this technique was combined with the use of small paper masks to cover

Left: *Shallow dish, 1740–60. Diameter 225 mm. Showing the use of a sponge to depict trees.*

Right: *Plate, 1740–60. Diameter 224 mm. Showing the use of a sponge for border patterns. Note that the painter forgot to insert the motif in reserve at 4 o'clock.*

Left: *Plate, 1740–60. Diameter 225 mm. Powdered blue with flower heads in reserves. Leaves scratched through.*

Right: *Plate, 1740–60. Diameter 222 mm. Powdered purple, with decoration in red.*

17

areas which could be decorated later. Powdered purple and blue were the most common, but 'dead leaf' brown, green and yellow are also known, while the areas initially covered by the masks (the reserves) were usually decorated in blue, rarely red.

Occasionally colours were outlined in a second, contrasting, colour – a procedure known as 'trekking', from the Dutch word *trekken*, 'to draw a line'. Another Dutch practice infrequently found on British delftware is the addition of a final clear lead glaze before the final firing, to give a bright, shiny finish.

Bianco sopra bianco ('white on white') decoration was probably introduced from Sweden in the 1730s and involved painting a pattern in dense white glaze around the rim of a plate or bowl against a strong blue background. The rest of the object could then be decorated, either in blue or in polychrome, typically with a pattern derived from oriental porcelain.

Above left: *Shallow bowl, 1740–60. Diameter 225 mm. Powdered purple with polychrome centre and motifs scratched through and painted in yellow.*

Above right: *Plate, 1760–70. Diameter 260 mm, with 'bianco sopra bianco' border. The landscape is European-inspired, the fishermen oriental.*

Left: *Plate, 1760–80. Diameter 223 mm. Delicate 'bianco sopra bianco' border. The colours in the centre have run, probably as a result of bad firing.*

Two processes were hardly ever used on tin-glazed earthenware: transfer printing and enamelling. It is surprising that transfer printing was so very little used as it was developed in Liverpool by Sadler and Green for the production of delftware tiles, but there are only a handful of pieces known to have been treated in this way. Enamelling (that is, painting with low-temperature colours on an already fired glaze) was much used on continental delftware but, although a few pieces were decorated in this way, it never caught on in Britain. The process required an additional firing and this increased the cost of production and the risk of damage in the kilns.

Above: *Two plates, both 1740–60, with the same design copied by two different painters. (Left) Diameter 223 mm. (Right) Diameter 263 mm, with 'bianco sopra bianco' border; the trees, in particular, much more carefully painted.*

Below: *Two plates, both 1750–70, with the same design copied by two different painters. (Left) Diameter 220 mm, painter's number '2' on reverse, decoration somewhat heavy-handed. (Right) Diameter 221 mm, painted more delicately with the same colours.*

Decorative styles

It is scarcely surprising that, as tin-glazed earthenware in England was begun by émigré craftsmen from the Low Countries, and in the absence of a local tradition, the decoration applied to the early pieces was stylistically identical to that of the Netherlands. It was, after all, the style they had been taught and which they, in their turn, were handing on to their apprentices. It was based on a variety of designs that could be traced back to the geometric patterns of Spanish (Hispano-Moresque) ceramics as they were developed through several centuries in Italy. The Italian potters had developed the *istoriato* style, the detailed scenes of mythological and historical subjects that were so popular with English collectors but these did not appear to any extent on Netherlands maiolica.

Thus the decoration that first appeared on English maiolica used all manner of geometric and star designs; pinwheels; rosettes and spirals; checkerboards; leaves and tendrils; flowers and fruits; and, to a lesser extent, animals and people. Fruits were particularly popular: pomegranates (often wrongly identified as apples), with or without bunches of grapes; less often oranges. Indeed, grapes occur on English ware right up to the end of the eighteenth century. Many types of flowers appear, the tulip predominating, although there are many examples of carnations, lilies, roses and daisies. Pieces decorated in the tradition of Netherlands maiolica were made throughout the seventeenth century, though as a declining proportion of the whole output, as new designs began to appear that had no real counterpart in the Netherlands.

The first of these was the 'royal' charger, bearing images of kings and queens, and other important though not royal personages. The second type was religiously inspired, notably pictures involving the

Left: *Charger, 1640–60. Diameter 331 mm. The central spiral merges into two concentric circles. The reverse has a whitish tin glaze.*

Below: *Charger, 1680–1700. Diameter 305 mm. Equestrian portrait of King William III.*

temptation with Adam, Eve, the serpent and the apple. Most of these can be traced back to an engraving by Crispin van de Passe of 1616 but, in the hands of the pot-painters, they were all too often anatomically grotesque. It is not surprising that in the Netherlands, where republicanism and anticlericalism held sway, such subjects should generally have been avoided, but they became very popular in England. A range of other

21

Two plates, 1760–5. Diameter 225 mm. Depicting Queen Charlotte and King George III. (By courtesy of Garry Atkins)

biblical and historical subjects appeared on English pieces and persisted as a decorative feature. From the middle of the seventeenth century we can find landscapes and houses that look like English rather than continental scenery.

Typically the edges of chargers – a large shallow dish with a heavy foot rim – were painted with a series of blue dashes (a border known in the Netherlands as 'cabled'), giving rise to the term 'blue-dash charger'. Very rarely, the dashes are in red.

The impact of oriental porcelain as it flooded into Europe began to show up in the decoration of British ware in the 1630s, when copies

Charger, 1680–1700. Diameter 338 mm. Sponged trees and blue dash border. Depicting the temptation of Adam and Eve. The reverse has a clear lead glaze.

22

Plate, 1630–50. Diameter 196 mm. With the 'bird on a rock' motif. (By courtesy of Jonathan Horne Antiques)

of the Chinese 'bird on a rock' design appeared on jugs, tankards and the like. Border patterns derived from oriental porcelain also appeared, sometimes fairly slavish copies of *kraak* (Chinese export porcelain) designs. These further copied oriental ware in being decorated in monochrome blue (sometimes with touches of purple), breaking away from the polychrome tradition of maiolica. The

Above: Plate, 1630–50. Diameter c.200 mm. With Chinese-inspired decoration and 'kraak' border.

Dish, 1710–30. Diameter 327 mm. Chinoiserie centre with 'kraak' border.

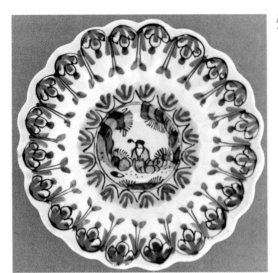

Moulded dish, 1680–1700. Diameter 221 mm. 'Chinaman among grasses' motif.

introduction of plates for table use in the second half of the seventeenth century was accompanied by the appearance of the 'Chinaman among grasses' motif that heralded the use of many similar motifs on all manner of pieces.

During the later years of the seventeenth century and the early years of the next a rapid growth in the output of tin-glazed earthenware took place; almost all of it was delftware, and maiolica disappeared. Many new designs were developed, with an increasing use of polychrome decoration. Much use was made of floral and foliage patterns, some going back to maiolica originals but

Saucer dish, 1740–60. Diameter 227 mm. A very European courting couple. (By courtesy of Jonathan Horne Antiques)

Plate, 1750–70. Diameter 222 mm. A couple in a European landscape.

increasingly copied from oriental porcelain. Some show distinctly Islamic influences. Mammals, fish and birds (rarely identifiable) often appear, as well as more and more landscapes, with or without figures. Other designs were of an overtly political character, such as those celebrating the Act of Union with Scotland of 1707. All manner of historical events were depicted, from the Battle of Culloden (1746) to the first balloon flights over London. Coats of arms, notably of London livery companies, regularly feature, particularly those of the Apothecaries' Company, which was naturally associated with the drug jars, pill slabs and the like

Above: *Plate, 1750–70. Diameter 214 mm. The depiction of foliage shows a decided Islamic influence.*

Bowl, 1740–60. Diameter 260 mm, height 100 mm. Pictures of country houses and gardens are quite common, but such a detailed depiction of a walled garden is rarely found. (By courtesy of David Cochrane)

that made up a staple of tin-glazed earthenware production.

Many of the decorative designs current right through the eighteenth century reflect the origin of delftware as a deliberate attempt to copy oriental porcelain. It is rare to find an exact copy of an oriental design, but most can be described as 'chinoiserie' – a western style of the seventeenth and eighteenth centuries, representing a fanciful interpretation of the original and featuring oriental motifs, asymmetrical forms and disturbed perspective. Motifs were borrowed and grouped without respect for their original context, and it is common to find oriental and European

Plate, 1750–70. Diameter 235 mm. European farming scene.

Plate, 1730–50. Diameter 226 mm. An example of a 'farmyard' design.

motifs together on the same piece, sometimes with amusing results. Many of the chinoiserie designs were done in monochrome blue, though they are often repeated in polychrome.

Among the oriental motifs used were hollow rocks (originally volcanic tufa), often used with little apparent understanding of what was being illustrated; Chinese fences, very distinctive and un-English; scrollwork, which appeared around 1695 and became a popular

Shallow bowl, c.1785. Diameter 225 mm. Commemorating a balloon flight, probably Blanchard's of 7th January 1785.

Right: Bowl, 1760–80. Diameter 230 mm, height 97 mm. Copy of a Chinese 'dragon' design.

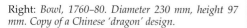

Dish, 1750–70. Diameter 340 mm. Birds with twisted necks are often found on chinoiserie delftware, but this one is eccentric by any standard.

Dish, 1740–60. Diameter 331 mm. A shard of this dish was dug up at the site of the Temple Back pot house in Bristol.

Right: Plate, 1750–70. Diameter 218 mm. Chinaman sitting on an English-type chair (with only two legs!).

Left: Plate, 1760–80. Diameter 223 mm. 'Long Lizzie' motif. The border has the cracked-ice motif and scratched-through elements.

Plate, 1740–60. Diameter 218 mm. Showing birds with typical twisted necks.

Plate, 1750–70. Diameter 235 mm. A copy of a well-known Chinese design.

Right: *Plate, 1740–60. Diameter 225 mm. Interesting use of multiple shades of blue.*

Left: *Plate, 1750–70. Diameter 223 mm. Note the insects, a frequently used motif.*

Plate, 1740–60. Diameter 227 mm. A mélange of chinoiserie motifs, with strutting bird.

Plate, 1760–80. Diameter 232 mm. Cracked-ice pattern, the Chinese symbol of spring.

Plate, 1780–1800. Diameter 229 mm. A late design, more appropriate to pearlware or porcelain.

border pattern; baskets of flowers, sometimes very debased; parasols; Chinamen fishing, either from a boat or from land; pagodas; birds, often with twisted necks; insects; elongated figures; and cracked ice, the Chinese symbol for spring.

Towards the end of the eighteenth century, when delftware was on the way out, a few new features appeared. These included floral swags round the rim, radial brush strokes inwards from the edge, and some designs that look forward to the decorative styles on pearlware and porcelain.

Marks and inscriptions

A number of different types of marks are found on the back of tin-glazed plates and dishes, and it is always worth turning a dish or plate over, if you can. The simplest type – numerals (usually, but by no means always, single figures) – are found in the centre of, or at least within, the foot ring. These are taken to be painters' marks, presumably for the calculation of piece-work. Similarly there are a few initials or other identification marks; these are rare, but the monogram 'WP', claimed to be the mark of William Pottery, a Bristol pot-painter and pot-house manager, is found on a few pieces, as is a trefoil floral rebus, said to be the mark of Joseph Flower, another

Bristol pot-painter. There are very few instances of potters signing their work, and very few pieces marked with an indication of the factory, though this can often be deduced from excavated wasters and other marks.

More often found are 'noughts and crosses' (*o* and *x* marks) and various brush strokes, usually eight of them, under the rim, more often on dishes but also sometimes on plates. No satisfactory explanation has yet been put forward for why they are there. Similarly there is a whole range of under-rim markings, variously described as ribbons, edge grasses,

Above: *Reverse of plate, 1750–70. Diameter 220 mm. With painter's number '2'.*

Reverse of dish, 1720–40. Diameter 332 mm. With monogram, presumed to be of William Pottery, and 'noughts and crosses'.

Plate, 1750–70. Diameter 225 mm. Showing under-rim ribbon marks and floral motif.

whiplashes and herbal sprigs. Again there seems to be no reason for their presence. Finally, a small group of plates is marked with a number of concentric circles.

The variety and number of inscriptions seem endless. Some are simple initials to identify a royal or other portrait – much needed, as many of the portraits are indistinguishable. Others are dates, with or without names or initials. Like all inscriptions, they can be on the front or back, or the inside or outside of a bowl or the like. Among the simplest descriptive inscriptions are those on wine bottles, marked 'Sack', 'Claret' or 'Whit' (that is, white), for example, usually dating from the 1640s and 1650s. Drinking seems to have inspired a range of inscriptions, including admonitions such as 'Drink fair, don't swear' (in a variety of spellings), 'Drinke and be mery', 'One bowl more and then', and longer messages: 'He that hath this cup in hand drinke up the beere let it not stand' (1656) or 'Drink drink whilst ye have breath for there is no drinking after death' (1756).

A number of different verses appear on puzzle jugs, of which the most frequent is:

> *Here gentlemen come try your skill*
> *I'll hold a wager if you will*
> *That you don't drink this liquor all*
> *Without you spill or let some fall.*

Other inscriptions celebrate births, such as 'Ann Wittin was born ye 14 of October 1717' (on a money box), or deaths: 'Near this place lies the body of Lucretia Bourne Anne daughter of

Wine bottle, dated 1644. Height 130 mm, diameter 85 mm.

Punch bowl, dated 1729. Diameter 300 mm, height 160 mm. With inscription 'Drink fair, Don't sware'.

Punch bowl, 1740–60. Diameter c.250 mm, height c.110 mm. Exhortations to drink are frequently found on punch bowls.

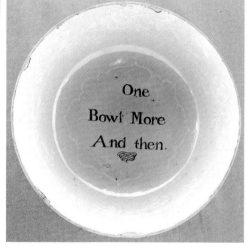

James and Edith Corfe who died Decr. 30 1755 aged 13 weeks' (on a panel). There are many marking weddings; these are often given as three initials in the form B^{A}C, where A is the initial of the surname, and B and C the initial of the first name of the husband and wife respectively. Sometimes both names are given in full.

Inscriptions concerning royalty, and particularly the rivalry between the Jacobites and Hanoverians, loom large, such as 'God save King George', 'God save ye Duke of Cumberland' (who crushed the 1745–6 Jacobite rebellion led by the Young Pretender at the decisive Battle of Culloden), 'Remember ye fight of Culloden', 'No pretender' or 'To the pious memory of Queen Anne, 1717', possibly Jacobite propaganda, as Queen Anne, the last of the Stuart kings and queens, had died in 1714.

Others are political, such as the many concerning John Wilkes, an MP seen as the champion of liberty and freedom of the press – 'Wilkes and liberty' or 'Honest Britons demand Wilkes' seate – 45'.

Above left: *Plate, dated 1687. Diameter 213 mm. Shows 'wedding' triangular mark at top, and line 6 from the Merryman verse. (By courtesy of the Potteries Museum and Art Gallery)*

Above right: *Punch bowl, 1760–80. Diameter 196 mm. Refers to issue no. 45 of Wilkes's weekly journal 'North Briton' (1762–3). (By courtesy of Jonathan Horne Antiques)*

There are also 'The Rt. Hon. William Pitt', 'Success to the British arms' and 'Admiral Keppel for ever' (Augustus Keppel, 1725–86, English admiral and politician). Another series relates to parliamentary elections, such as 'Calvert and Martin for ever' (for the Tewkesbury election of 1754). All of these seem to refer to elections in the West Country.

One of the most famous inscriptions on English tin-glazed

Plate, 1750–1800. Diameter 230 mm. Used to support a candidate for parliamentary election. (By courtesy of the Potteries Museum and Art Gallery)

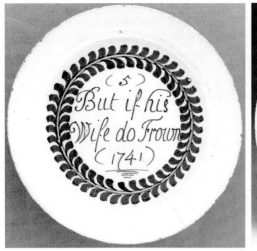

Above left: *Plate, dated 1741. Diameter 193 mm. With line 5 of the Merryman verse.*

Above right: *Punch bowl, 1750–70. Diameter 195 mm. Probably relates to the Seven Years' War (1756–63), in which Britain fought France over colonial territories in the New World and Far East. (By courtesy of Jonathan Horne Antiques)*

earthenware comes on the earliest dated dish, now in the Museum of London, with the date variously read as 1600 or 1602. The painter has taken the couplet

> *The rose is red, the leaves are greene*
> *God save Elizabeth our noble queene*

and shortened it by omitting *noble* before *queene*, presumably to make it fit into the available space.

A frequently found rhyme is the so-called Merryman set, where each line of a six-line stanza appears on a separate plate, usually within a cartouche. The whole reads:

> 1. *What is a merryman*
> 2. *Let him do what he can*
> 3. *To entertain his guests*
> 4. *With wine and merry jests*
> 5. *But if his wife doth frown*
> 6. *All merriment goes down.*

Spelling is often unorthodox, and complete sets – each line with the same date – are rare.

There are many more types of inscription: arms and mottoes of city livery companies; other armorials; *memento mori* ('You and I are earth'); wishing prosperity ('To the flocks', 'To the Borough of Lewis', for example); patriotic ('Awake O Brittons now awake, stand to your glorious arms, and make the Frenchmans' hearts quake, for

insults and alarms'); and those on barbers' bowls ('Sir, your quarters up', when payment was due). There are some traps for the unwary, however, as some Dutch Delft plates have English inscriptions; they were made to celebrate couples (presumably on marriage) in coastal East Anglia.

Probably the most interesting of all the inscriptions are those on 'ship bowls' – punch bowls, mostly from Liverpool, made to celebrate journeys of ships from that port, many of them engaged in the round trip Liverpool – West Africa – America – Liverpool. These bowls have an impressively detailed and nautically accurate portrayal of a ship, its rigging, sails and armament, and in a ribbon underneath there is a message, such as 'Success to the Gainsborough, Brockelbank Master'. One bowl goes further: 'Success to trade and navigation and may they ever in triumph ride upon the surface of the wave'.

The interest of all these inscriptions lies not so much in themselves as in the light they shed upon the society of their time and the way in which life is reflected in everyday utensils.

Attribution

It is often difficult to identify the factory – or even group of factories – at which a piece of tin-glazed earthenware was made. Only with a great deal of experience based on examination and handling can a reasonable determination be put forward, and the reader is referred to the large-scale museum monographs for further study. Attribution is too complicated for a book of this scope, and for that reason it has not been discussed.

For early pieces it is even difficult to distinguish Netherlands from English origin, since both were made by Netherlands-trained potters. The only sure way is by chemical analysis of the body, a technique with which the British Museum specialists have made remarkable contributions in recent years, but this approach has not yet been used to identify work from different British factories. For this, the most secure basis is the study of wasters and shards recovered from excavations of factory sites, but even this is not foolproof, as you may be looking at broken pieces of something 'bought in'. Even so, a great deal of identification is now established and can be explored further.

The difficulty of secure attribution arises from several considerations: the use of relatively few shared sources of clay in different places; the narrow range of pigments available; the same sources of decoration used everywhere; and, above all, the well-documented movement of turners and painters between factories.

Dating is, by comparison, less difficult as, apart from specific decoration that can be related to known historical events, there are hundreds of pieces carrying a date that may usually be assumed to reflect the date of manufacture. These can be used for comparative study.

Dish, 1720–40. Diameter 332 mm. The reverse of this dish, with the monogram of William Pottery, is illustrated on page 31 (bottom).

A note for collectors

It is still quite possible to build up a representative collection of English tin-glazed earthenware without vast expenditure, though rare and beautiful pieces achieve very high prices in the sale rooms. All the major auction houses regularly feature pieces in their sales, and often lots of four to six plates can be examined on viewing days and sometimes bought quite reasonably. There are several specialist dealers in London, whose knowledge and experience is willingly shared with collectors, and visits to good antique fairs usually turn up a number of examples. Polychrome pieces are naturally more eye-catching and tend to be more expensive than blue and white, but the latter should not be neglected as they often carry the more interesting decorative designs.

Collectors have to make up their minds what attitude to take to damage and repairs, since few pieces have come down to us in perfect condition. Chipped edges are the rule rather than the exception, and cracks extending some way into, if not right across, a piece are frequent. Unless edge chips obscure the border pattern to such an extent that the eye keeps being drawn to them, they are perhaps best left as they are. Cracks should be consolidated before they spread and open out. Painting and above all spraying are best avoided unless done so expertly as to be invisible, but remember that a damaged piece, however skilfully repaired, remains a damaged piece. Some older repairs that used inappropriate adhesives, and where repairers' paintwork has begun to change colour, can be horrible to look at and are best avoided; if such pieces are bought it may be best to have the old work stripped off and done again. In general, repairs to tin-glazed earthenware can be quite tricky and should be left to the experienced specialist.

Above all, remember that a damaged piece is no less interesting, or less rare, than its perfect counterpart. Whether you want to have it in your collection depends on your point of view. The inherent fragility of tin-glazed earthenware ensures that, as time goes by, perfect pieces will become harder and harder to find.

Bowl, 1740–60.
Diameter 250 mm.
Chinese-style landscape
in blue and purple.

Further reading

Archer, M. *Delftware: The Tin-Glazed Earthenware of the British Isles*. HMSO, 1997.

Atkins, G. *Annual Exhibitions of English Pottery*. Catalogues, 1991– .

Austin, J.C. *British Delftware at Williamsburg*. Colonial Williamsburg Foundation, 1994.

Britton, F. *English Delftware in the Bristol Collection*. Sotheby, 1982.

Britton, F. *London Delftware*. Jonathan Horne, 1987.

Caiger-Smith, A. *Tin-Glazed Pottery in Europe and the Islamic World*. Faber, 1973.

Francis, P. *Irish Delftware*. Jonathan Horne, 2000.

Garner, F.H., and Archer, M. *English Delftware*. Faber, 1972.

Grigsby, L.B. *The Longridge Collection of English Slipware and Delftware: Volume 2, Delftware*. Jonathan Horne, 2000.

Horne, J. *A Collection of Early English Pottery*. Catalogues, 1980– .

Lipski, L.L., and Archer, M. *Dated English Delftware: Tin-Glazed Earthenware, 1600–1800*. Sotheby, 1984.

Ray, A. *English Delftware Pottery in the Robert Hall Warren Collection, Ashmolean Museum, Oxford*. Faber, 1968.

Ray, A. *English Delftware in the Ashmolean Museum*. Jonathan Horne, 2000.

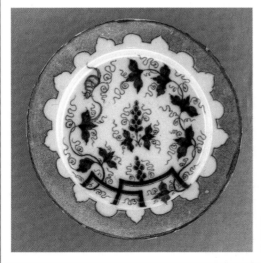

Dish, 1740–60. Diameter 354 mm. Powdered purple, with chinoiserie decoration in blue.

Places to visit

Many museums have pieces of tin-glazed earthenware, but those listed here have important collections. Readers are advised to contact museums and galleries before visiting to check opening times.

Allen Gallery, 10–12 Church Street, Alton, Hampshire GU34 2BW. Telephone: 01420 82802. Website: www.hants.gov.uk/museum/allen/index.html

Ashmolean Museum, Beaumont Street, Oxford OX1 2PH. Telephone: 01865 278000. Website: www.ashmol.ox.ac.uk

Bristol City Museum and Art Gallery, Queen's Road, Bristol BS8 1RL. Telephone: 0117 922 3571. Website: www.bristol-city.gov.uk/museums

Fitzwilliam Museum, Trumpington Street, Cambridge CB2 1RB. Telephone: 01223 332900. Website: www.fitzmuseum.cam.ac.uk

Liverpool Museum, William Brown Street, Liverpool L3 8EN. Telephone: 0151 478 4399. Website: www.nmgm.org.uk

Museum of London, 150 London Wall, London EC2Y 5HN. Telephone: 020 7600 3699. Website: www.museum-london.org.uk

Potteries Museum and Art Gallery, Bethesda Street, Hanley, Stoke-on-Trent ST1 3DE. Telephone: 01782 232323. Website: www.stoke.gov.uk/museums

Victoria and Albert Museum, Cromwell Road, South Kensington, London SW7 2RL. Telephone: 020 7942 2000. Website: www.vam.ac.uk

Bowl, 1760–80. Diameter 230 mm. European-type landscape in blue.